Game Plan
for
Getting Published

Game Plan
for
Getting Published

A Handbook for Non-fiction Authors

Maryann Karinch

ARMINLEAR

Cover Design by C.S. Fritz

ISBN: 978-1-7351698-8-0

Armin Lear Press
825 Wildlife
Estes Park, CO 80517

Table of Contents

Introduction: You Asked for It

Ever since my first book came out in December 1994, I have received notes and calls from people who ask: "How do I get published?" The first response I gave in those early days is: Write about what you know. Or, if you are an amazing writer who doesn't know anything, find yourself an expert who either doesn't write well or doesn't have the time to write and team up with that person.

I saw the downside of that advice nine years later when I founded my literary agency.

Downside? But isn't that classic advice, given by every writing teacher on the planet?

Yes, it is. Nonetheless, it's "half-advice." Many decent writers have heard that message and conclude they should write about their lives. Let me give you a frightening example of what this reasoning can lead to: a memoir submitted to me by a 24-year-old woman who chronicled the pain of two failed relationships in 115,000 words.

So, it's true that you're the only one who lived your life and that qualifies you to write about it, however, there are lots of readers who probably would not find your life interesting. The downside of the advice, therefore, is that you can write what you know, and no one will care enough to read your sentences.

The second half of the advice is equally important: Write to fill a hole—a hole in your reader's awareness, knowledge, convictions, or emotional life.

The rest of this book responds to questions and confusions that plague authors who want to have a commercial publisher applaud their talent and offer them a contract. Every week, I receive so many questions about getting published, and see so much confusion about the process of publishing, that I run out of "teaching time." That's the reason for doing this book. If you want my guidance, here it is. If you also want guidance from some of my distinguished colleagues (from whom I have learned much), start with books by Jeff Herman, and then see what other offerings are near his books on the shelves an in online listings of similar works.

Before unleashing my judgments and humor in the upcoming pages, I wanted to share my background with you in 147 words so that you know who I am and why I can help you.

While earning a BA in speech and drama, I discovered a love of writing—thanks to my friend and accomplished journalist, Patti Mengers, who pursued me to write for our college newspaper. During graduate school, I discovered the skill of writing—thanks to Dr. Gary Williams, who rejected my work when it fell short and coached me toward excellence. In developing my first book, I discovered the profession of writing—thanks to Dr. Joan Dunphy at New Horizon Press, who pushed for "better" and helped me figure out how to deliver it. When she died, my heart broke; she became my friend and helped shape my career. Now that I've had 32 books commercially published by 15 different houses of all sizes and made deals with houses of all sizes for 150 authors, most of whom were first-timers, I feel I have practical advice to offer you.

I cite these phases of development and these names of real people to reinforce a critical point with you: Mentors make a difference. They help you through the stages of progress—stages that include painful failures in most cases—and they make you realize that success is attainable.

Through this book, I hope to be your mentor.

Part I: The Query Letter

Chapter 1: Why Would I Say "No!" after Reading Your Query Letter?

'Twas the day before Christmas and a hundred emails flooded my inbox. Amid the specials on boxed pears and running shoes were seven query letters. They had such holiday themes as the disintegration of Western civilization, the shameful treatment of Native Americans, a child's murder, the plight of struggling screenwriters, modern aviation, living with a crippling disease, and how God and baseball belong together. Two of the letters stood out as well-written, provocative, and reflecting a good sense of the market; I invited proposals.

Every day of the year, query letters show up electronically. On rare occasions, they even show up in the mail. (I discourage using the mail because we must do business electronically, from query to contract to final edits of a book.) On big holidays, like Christmas and Independence Day, I might get only one or two queries. A typical business day's reading involves between ten and twenty letters, plus an additional three or four complete proposals. This constitutes heavy volume for me since I am also an active author.

Because you probably know about this volume of queries already, or at least have suspected it, your first question might be "How do I make it past the first read?"

Here are the *logical* reasons I pass on a project—or a person—based on the query letter alone:

1. Not a genre we handle. At the moment, the agency doesn't represent children's books,

poetry, screenplays, or religious books. This information about the agency can be found easily online at multiple sites. When in doubt—conflicting information can occur on different websites, depending on when they are updated—a one-line note asking if we still have a policy about not handling a particular genre is a thoughtful action.

2. An incoherent or unfocused query. Here's what that might look like:

In the middle of the night, it occurred to me that my life is interesting. Not to everyone, but to the millions of people who watch reality TV every week. My life is like a really good reality TV show, with biting spiders and kids fighting and cakes falling apart. As Mark Twain said, "Be good and you will be lonesome." Are you interested in my life story?

Consider how hard it is to write a polite and encouraging response to something like that.

3. No credentials. If you propose to refute Einstein's Theory of Relativity, you should either have a few degrees in physics or a co-author who has a few degrees in physics. As I said in the Introduction, "Write what you know" is one half of a reliable axiom. If your query does not make it clear you are following that advice, then either rethink the project or re-write the query. A common misperception about credentials comes from the belief that living through an event or situation makes you an expert in it. Having an autistic child does not make you an expert in autism, but it does, very likely, make you an expert on the day-to-day demands of nurturing an autistic child.

4. The project has been shopped around already. Whether you shopped it around yourself or another agent did it, when you come to me after your proposal has already hit dozens of editors' desks, I don't want it. Go back and rethink your project, and then come back after you give it new life—and a new title.

5. The project has been self-published. Unless you have had blockbuster sales and a cult following (a la *Fifty Shades of Grey*), I can't get a publisher interested in a previously self-published project. Take down the Amazon page, take sales of it off your website, and pretend it never happened before you come to me.

Here are the *emotional* reasons I pass on a project—or a person—based on the query letter alone:

1. Leading with insults, or "You're slime like everyone else; represent me." This is the most baffling approach of all, and I see versions of it regularly. The author has a monumental cause and, if I support it by representing her book, then I can escape my ignominious existence. The letter begins something like this: "Since you have plenty to eat, you probably don't care about kids with rickets . . ." Somewhere at the bottom of the page is the heartwarming close: "But you can redeem yourself by representing this project." During the mid-pandemic protests over racism in law enforcement practices, I even got approached with, "You're a white woman so you probably will discriminate against a brown man." Bottom line: No, I won't.

2. Pushing genius. Often, the author com-

pares himself to a well-known writer to establish a clear perception of his greatness. One time, an author took great care in comparing himself to Jack Kerouac. "Dear John," I replied, "I can't stand *On the Road.*"

3. An expressed guarantee that the work will be a bestseller. "A sure thing—you'd be a fool not to take it on! You want to make money, don't you?" Usually such statements precede a caveat: "All I need is the backing of a major publishing house..." And if every author who optimistically described her chances of appearing on *Today* actually got to sit on that stage in New York, there would be no time in my day for the women who think they've made love with aliens.

4. A broadcast query. If I sent a broadcast query to 53 editors about your project, how do you think they would respond? To put it bluntly, I might as well shut down the agency the moment I hit the "send" button. In talking with my colleagues in the business, most admit they don't even reply to a broadcast query. They consider it spam.

5. Careless communication. "Hey, Maryann, like I really like the fact that you live in the mountains and it's probably cool there in the summer—I mean *literally* cool—because you're so high. You know, I don't mean like really high because you're in Colorado, I just mean high up."

Chapter 2: Why Would I Say "Yes" after Reading Your Query Letter?

You catch my attention because you address a handful of information needs in fewer than 300 words.

Here is what I want to see in the query; each of these concepts receives more attention in Chapter 3 when I talk about proposal contents:

- Genre. State what category your book fits into. It's fine to list a primary category as well as a secondary one. Please go to Publishers Marketplace or at the very least, go to Amazon and note the classifications of books. It does not help your case to say that it crosses genres. I cringe when I see something like this: "It's a memoir, but more than that, it's a how-to book about losing weight, and it could easily fit into nutrition, pop psychology or pop culture because I do a lot on YouTube."

- Expertise. Make it clear why you are qualified to write this book. In the world of publishing, your academic credentials and professional experience are still important. Publishing is not social media; be prepared to document your expertise.

- Professionalism. Treat the query like business correspondence. I have a name and it isn't Agent, as in "Dear Agent." You have an address and phone number in addition to your email address, so state them. Indicate that you are prepared to provide a complete proposal. It's frustrating to get a provocative query letter and then have to wait two months for the author to complete a proposal—not only that, but it makes me question whether the person has the ability to meet production deadlines.

• Platform. Although having an established platform isn't always a requirement, it is with most projects. Publishers want assurances that you can promote your book, and in the context of describing your platform, you make it clear who your target audiences are and how you have the proven ability to reach them. Platform = ability to drive sales.

• Writing style. Put yourself into the query. The query letter is like meeting me at the hors d'oeuvres table. Please greet me with the same care you would invest in a face-to-face meeting.

The following is a sample query letter that would interest me. It is fabricated, by the way:

Dear Maryann,

My husband stole $5 million, but he didn't know it. A brilliant neonatologist, Sam suffers from Dissociative Identity Disorder, which used to be known as multiple personality disorder. He could play a round of golf, go on a two-week trip, or defraud insurance companies over the course of several months and not remember what he did.

My 13 Husbands is my completed memoir about the man, crime, and decade-long marriage I had with Sam and his dozen "alters." Since Sam's recent incarceration, I have been a guest on *The View* and maintained a blog for *Psychology Today*. I have started speaking to women's organizations of all sizes and am scheduled to be part of a main-stage panel at a mental health conference with more than 1,000 attendees. I will seek every opportunity possible to share my insights and experiences and intend to leverage my status as a faculty member at Kent State to find opportunities to do so.

Above all, my book is an engaging personal story—a memoir with a narrative arc. Tucked inside it are facts about an extreme mental illness that allow people to perform at high levels. Britney Spears, who has had the spotlight shine on her own mental health challenges, told me she will offer an endorsement.

Thank you for your consideration. I have prepared a complete proposal and would be pleased to forward it at your request in Word or PDF format.

Sincerely,

Sue Smith

Dr. Susan Smith
1212 Hummingbird Feeder Lane
Kent, Ohio 44242
330.555.1212
susansmithfashionprof@tsrajsofdam.edu

This sample query letter meets all the criteria outlined in the bullets in a mere 238 words.

Part II: The Proposal

Chapter 3: Anatomy of a Proposal

This chapter includes a sample proposal, but in the subsequent chapters in this section, I take that proposal apart. I also offer you specific guidance on tailoring the format to your needs. I wanted you to see a proposal in its entirety first to get a sense of flow and build.

But first: Why do you have to do a proposal for a work of non-fiction?

Experts, particularly people in the academic community, hit me with snotty comments all the time when I ask for a proposal. "You're supposed to do that!" (Thanks for the job description, Dr. Dude.) Or, "I've already completed the manuscript; I'm past the proposal stage!"

Think about your proposal as preparation for a job interview. You have an opportunity, research it, and prepare to meet with the gatekeeper at the organization who is hiring. A career coach (*aka* agent) helps you prepare. Get past the gatekeeper (*aka* acquisitions editor), and you will be a giant step closer to a job. The gatekeeper needs to know enough about you and your qualifications that he can march into a room full of people who don't want to spend money on you and argue, "This one is pure gold to us."

In theory, you know your project better than anyone. As an agent, I can and will help you improve your proposal, but you have a responsibility to do your best in composing the first draft. Believe me, if a reputable agent invites a proposal from you, that person is already seriously interested in your project. When she sees that you can deliver a strong draft, she will work overtime to help you take it to the next level.

My logic in organizing the components of the proposal is that I want you to open with clear case for the merits of the project from an editorial and marketing perspective. Each section should build on the next. By the time the acquisitions editor reads your sample material, you should have already convinced him or her that this project belongs in the marketplace. After that, it's a matter of how well you write.

When an agent invites a proposal from you, you might say that you have prepared a proposal, but would appreciate knowing if that agent's requirements differ from *Game Plan for Getting Published*, or whatever proposal guidelines you have followed. We have slightly different ways of presenting the case, so it's best if you know what the agent wants to see. Generally, it's best to stick to one simple font, double-spaced, although you may want to vary a little bit for the title or tables and charts. Avoid putting in high resolution images, which will make the file extremely large.

I recommend avoiding very large (like 14-point Times New Roman) or very small (like 10-point Times New Roman) type. I have noticed that very small type tends to be a proposal from a young person and large type tends to be a proposal from an old person. Do you want to be typed that way before your work is even read?

The flow of the proposal I rely on is as follows:

Overview – Bait

The Market – Who will buy the book?

Promotion Plan/Platform – How will you reach

those people? How are you reaching them now?

Competitive Analysis – What are they buying now, and why will they buy your book in addition to or instead of those other books?

Author Bio – What about your experience and education make you the best person to write and promote this book?

Table of Contents – At first glance, what makes this book interesting?

Chapter-by-Chapter Synopsis – Now that I'm interested, what else should I know that will make me want to read this book?

Sample Material – The part that earns you the title "author"

You might also want to include as Appendices curriculum vitae if you're a physician or scientist, or a concise collection of media clips if you've been interviewed a lot. Just make sure that whatever you put in the proposal is necessary to make your case. Padding a proposal wastes everyone's time.

The sample proposal below was created for a project that was published in 2005 under a different title. It went on to sell hundreds of thousands of copies worldwide. It was so successful, in fact, that the publisher had us do a second edition in 2012. I also want you to pay attention to the fact that the book described in this proposal ultimately led to success in foreign markets as well as domestic. Among the translations/ foreign rights licensed by our US publisher to date are to publishers in China, Arabic speaking nations, Malaysia, Singapore, Greece, Turkey, Vietnam, Poland, Korea, the United Kingdom, Canada, Germany, Brazil,

France, India, Australia, Portugal, Russia, Bulgaria, and Japan. Foreign and translation rights are important for an author in this global economy. When you craft your proposal, think about how your book would appeal to a global market.

View this sample proposal for format and general content only. I've intentionally chosen a proposal from a long time ago because (a) you won't be inclined to steal from it and (b) the basic format has stood the test of time.

After the proposal, I've included the Table of Contents from the published work so that you have the benefit of seeing an evolution from proposal stage to completion of the project. You can see two outcomes from this presentation:

1. How the authors' thinking about the content evolved.

2. How interaction with a good editor helped the material to evolve. In this case, it was input from both the acquisitions editor, Michael Pye, and the developmental editor, Kirsten Dalley, that helped the work take shape.

The result is that the book became a hit I the United States and in the countries mentioned above.

Although as an agent I am happy to work with different structures, this sample proposal lays out the basics of what publishers need to know to decide whether or not they want to acquire your book.

CAUTION: Do not draw directly from material in this sample—some facts have been replaced with lies to protect the intellectual property of those of us who wrote it!

Make Them Tell the Truth

Using Interrogation Secrets in Love and Business

Greg Hartley and Maryann Karinch

Proposal Contents

Make Them Tell the Truth
Using Interrogation Secrets in Love and Business

Greg Hartley and Maryann Karinch

Overview

Greg Hartley has the trust of the US and UK governments in conducting interrogation training for intelligence and law enforcement personnel. His insights have been featured on ABC, Fox, CNN, CNBC, The History Channel, MSNBC, and in *The Washington Post*, among others. He trained Chris Mackey, author of *The Interrogators: Inside the Secret War Against al Qaeda*, and many other top professionals who are putting their skills to use to break Saddam Hussein and the prisoners held at Guantanamo.

With Maryann Karinch, author of eight works of non-fiction, Greg Hartley now brings the tricks of the trade to all people who want a little more truth in their lives.

Who needs *Make Them Tell the Truth*? Anyone with a cheating spouse or manipulative boss. Anyone conducting job interviews or cold-calling prospective customers. Anyone trying to survive the dating scene or faced with a string of business meetings with clients. Anyone who has teenagers at home or works on Capitol Hill. Well, pretty much anyone.

The Market

Why does *Desperate Housewives* draw an average of 21.8 million viewers every week? In part, to catch the drama of cheating and lying. People are fascinated with arts of both deception and detection. Of course, the desperate lives of the women on Wisteria Lane wouldn't be nearly as interesting if they had professional interrogation skills. But ask real "housewives" and they are likely to tell you that they would rather have those skills in their arsenal of happy homemaking than the traumatic life of a soap character.

The market for this book is people in love and business who do not want to be taken advantage of by deceptive people. It is people who want to understand human behavior well enough to debate productively, improve their own style of communication, and not be duped by people around them, whether they know them well or hardly know them.

In addition to the millions of men and women who think their spouse or partner is cheating on them, prime market segments from the business world include the following (there is some overlap of categories):

Occupation	US total
Sales	1.4 million
Management	6.6 million
(hiring/firing, supervisory roles)	
Legal	951,510
Business & financial operations	4.9 million
(insurance, banks)	

Promotion

A sampling of Greg Hartley's recent media appearances suggests what we will be able to do to promote *Make Them Tell the Truth*. (This lists domestic media only.) In addition to leveraging Greg's connections with TV and radio show producers, as well as print and online journalists, Maryann Karinch will exploit her 20 years of experience in public relations and interview relationships with NPR; her connections will support a multi-media campaign that puts Greg in the spotlight.

ABC

ABC Nightly News	"What is allowed in Interrogation?"
ABC News Nightline	"Should we torture?"
ABCNews.com	"Iraqi Abuse Scandal May Affect Terror War"05/11/2004

FOX

KTLA News   5/11/2004

Fox And Friends

Four appearances on: AbuGhraib Scandal
                                              (05/09/2004)
Intelligence failures   (06/11/2004)
The Najaf Situation   (08/26/04)
Torture during Interrogation   (12/04/04)

CNN

CNN Live Saturday	"Effective Interrogation"
CNN International	"Effective Interrogation: The making of an interrogator"

MSNBC *Countdown with Keith Olbermann*
Abu Ghraib and Interrogation

NPR *Talk of the Nation*

Abuse of the Iraqi prisoners 05/03/04

The History Channel "We Can Make You Talk"

Philadelphia Enquirer Abu Ghraib 5/6/2004

Washington Post "The Abu Ghraib Scandal" 05/11/2004

Competition

First of all, books on lie detection are selling well. After selecting a few competitive titles, we realized that they (a) are still moving after being on the shelves three to five years, (b) omit some of the most important skills in detecting deception in daily life, for example, baselining, and (c) don't address the flip side of the topic, that is, self-defense.

Effective Interviewing and Interrogation Techniques (Academic Press; 1st edition, 2001) by Nathan J. Gordon, William L. Fleisher, C. Donald Weinberg is a steady seller despite this slim volume's (192 pages) hefty price of $69.95 and age. The book purports to offer a practical, straightforward method for interviewing witnesses and victims, interrogating suspects, and accurately identifying them as truthful or untruthful. Clearly, then, the primary audience is not consumers, but rather law enforcement and related professionals. Unlike *Make Them Tell the Truth*, this book is focused on the methodical extraction of information though a formal "ritualized" interrogation. Our concept is to adapt the concepts used by interrogators into a real-world application for daily life.

With a list price of $12, Jef Nance's *Conquering Deception* (Irvin Benham Group, 2001) is clearly aimed at a consumer market. Unfortunately, this "handbook for the savvy conversationalist" takes the shortcut of teaching absolutes regarding the meaning of certain gestures and eye movements. *Make Them Tell the Truth* teaches the mechanics of why things happen, how to detect stress, and how signals of deception may vary from person to person.

Never Be Lied To Again: How to Get the Truth In 5 Minutes Or Less In Any Conversation Or Situation (St. Martin's Griffin,1999) by David J. Lieberman has a premise that puts it in the realm of party trick, like a five-minute cure for claustrophobia. Lieberman relies on techniques in hypnosis and psycholinguistics to teach people to influence someone to tell the truth. *Make Them Tell the Truth* is not about a miraculous tool that allows you to force people to tell the truth immediately. Our concept is taking a proven set of tools, explaining how they work, why they work, and how to use them. Our tools will become more useful as you practice them both in making people tell the truth and improving your own communication skills and self-control.

In important ways, Paul Ekman's *Telling Lies: Clues to Deceit in the Marketplace, Politics, and Marriage* (W.W. Norton & Company; 2nd, Rev. edition, 2001) is more complementary than competitive. Ekman examines the deception strategies of international public figures, such as Adolf Hitler and Richard Nixon, as well as the deceitful behavior of private individuals, including adulterers and petty criminals. This is a study aimed mainly at law enforcement and related professions, but its success might indicate that the $15.95 price and content make it attractive to consumers as well. Our concept is not case studies, but rather interpretations of tools used by professional interrogators to daily life applications. Our intent is to provide a system for motivating the truth and a system for baselining to determine honest behavior. In addition, *Make Them Tell the Truth* addresses the important topic of self-defense against tactics of lying and interrogation.

Authors' Bios: Greg Hartley and Maryann Karinch

Gregory Hartley's expertise as an interrogator first earned him honors with the United States Army. More recently, it has drawn organizations such as the Defense Intelligence Agency, Navy SEALS, Federal law enforcement agencies, and national TV to seek his insights about "how to" as well as "why."

Hartley has an illustrious military record. He graduated from the U.S. Army Interrogation School, the Anti-Terrorism Instructor Qualification Course, the Principle Protection Instructor Qualification Course, several Behavioral Symptom Analysis Seminars, and SERE (Survival, Evasion, Resistance, Escape) school. His skills as an expert interrogator earned praise while he served as SERE Instructor, Operational Interrogation Support to the 5th Special Forces Group during operation Desert Storm, Interrogation Trainer, and as a creator and director of several joint-force, multi-national interrogation exercises from 1994 to 2000. Among his military awards are the Meritorious Service Medal (2x), Army Commendation Medal (5x), Army Achievement Medal (4x), National Defense Service Medal, Southwest Asia Service Medal, and Kuwait Liberation Medal. He also attended law school at Rutgers University.

Hartley has provided expert interrogation analysis for major network and cable television, as well as National Public Radio and prime print media such as *The Washington Post* and *Philadelphia Enquirer*. Important foreign media such as *Der Spiegel* have also relied on his commentary.

Hartley is currently a partner and consultant for Team Delta, a company that specializes in training corporate America and law enforcement using skills derived from the interrogation process.

Maryann Karinch is the author of the following books:

Dr. David Sherer's Hospital Survival Guide (co-author David Sherer, MD, Claren Books, 2003) offers an insider's guide to making your hospital stay safe and comfortable.

Rangers Lead the Way: The Army Rangers' Guide to Leading Your Organization Through Chaos (co-author Dean Hohl, Adams Media, 2003) describes how to apply the principles and techniques of U.S. Army Ranger training to the business environment.

Diets Designed for Athletes (Human Kinetics, 2001) guides athletes, coaches, and trainers in choosing the best whole foods and supplements to enhance performance.

Empowering Underachievers: How to Guide Failing Kids (8-18) to Personal Excellence (co-author Dr. Peter Spevak, New Horizon Press, 2000) offers both theory and practical to-do advice from a leading expert on helping underachieving kids get "unstuck."

Lessons from the Edge: Extreme Athletes Show You How to Take on High Risk and Succeed (Simon & Schuster, 2000) features extreme sports heroes: world-record holders, gold medalists, adventurers. It includes their dramatic stories and conditioning secrets.

Boot Camp: The Sergeant's Fitness and Nutrition Program (co-author Patrick "The Sarge" Avon, Simon & Schuster, 1999) is a fitness and nutrition program designed to help readers "Be All You Used to Be™" that uses quick-witted, military style humor.

Telemedicine: What the Future Holds When You're Ill (New Horizon Press, 1994) looks at the role of technology in transforming healthcare around the world.

She wrote *Navigating the Mortgage Maze* (Holt/ Owl) for Andrew E. Turnauer, named one of the ten best real estate books of 1997.

As a communications consultant, she has designed media and marketing programs for companies, associations, and individuals. She also managed public relations for Apple Computer's federal division. As Director of Communications for an industry trade group composed of high-tech leaders, she served as a spokesman on legislative and regulatory issues. Prior to that she managed a professional theater in Washington, DC. She holds Bachelor's and Master's degrees from The Catholic University of America in Washington, DC.

Table of Contents

Introduction: Who is this book for?

Section I: Context

Section II: Tools

(c) Minimizing

Section III: Applying the Tools in Love

7. Fight to get what you want

8. Extract the truth

9. Change the way you fight to make the relationship better

10. Are you in captivity, not love?

Section IV: Applying the Tools to Business

11. Direct a job interview

     (a) Interviewer

     (b) Interviewee

12. Get the upper hand in a meeting

     (c) One-on-one

     (d) Small meeting

     (e) Large meeting

13. Close the deal or make the sale

     (f) Cold calls

     (g) Building on prior contact

Section V: Self-Defense

14. How to avoid falling for these techniques

Conclusion: Respect your new power

Chapter-by-Chapter Synopsis

Introduction: Who is this book for?

Have you ever been lied to? Of course. Have you ever been lied to by a spouse? A business partner? A parent? Your boss? Your child? If you haven't, then close the book. You've managed to surround yourself with radically honest people. (There may be a dozen somewhere on earth.)

As for the rest of the world, this book is for you.

Rather than think of this as a handbook for catching someone in the act of deception (which it is) you might want to think of it as a primer on human behavior. Men and women, adults and children, athletes and sedentary folks—what you are genetically, chronologically, and habitually shapes how you think and behave. This book will deepen your understanding of the differences between people so that you can use them to understand other people. At the same time, you get the added advantage of learning to control your own behavior. In effect, you become better at figuring out other people while you become more inscrutable.

In this book, you will get:

- The basics on who lies and why.
- How your brain works

    - If your brain normally does x under stress it will do y.

- Symptoms of stress, as a sign of deception.
- Applications to daily life of seeing stress in someone else
- With people you know intimately
- With people you hardly know, or don't know

at all

• Ways to block others from detecting your stress

Section I: Context

1. Where do these techniques come from? (or, What does Abu Ghraib have to do with you?)

This chapter introduces readers to the world of professional interrogators in such a way that regular people can easily see how the techniques of this elite corps can apply to daily life.

Sample information:

The stressors that make a soldier come undone can also make a person in a bad relationship come undone. And "relationship" can mean marriage, business, fraternity, or any other group in which we fancy monkeys play politics with each other.

You've no doubt heard stories of hard-charging soldiers who died at enemy hands because they refused to talk. For them the most sacred part of themselves, that little box inside that contained their core identity, was their duty to protect others' lives by protecting certain information. Everyone has a little box. You may not even know what it contains, but if you lose it, you face a kind of personal extinction.

An excellent interrogator—and few of that calibre even exist—will identify what's in that box and use it to break you. With words, the interrogator creates a threat worse than the threat of death. It's worse because you would lose the one thing you can't afford to lose: What makes you *you*.

2. Why and how do people lie?

"Honey, do these pants make my butt look big?"

"No. But your butt sure makes those pants look small."

People often indulge in minor levels of deception to avoid hurting someone's feelings, but outright lying is a different matter. There are web sites that help people lie about cheating on a spouse or to a boss about not showing up for work. The people who run them have made lying a profession; they have focused on transgressions that very likely involve the "need" to lie.

Insecurities also drive some people to lie. Your date fabricates a story about spending time in Paris so you think she's more cosmopolitan. You uncle invents a tour of duty in Vietnam so people think he's tough.

Shredding a lie that is not just an embellishment of truth may take very little skill: Ask enough questions and, at some point, the story breaks down. But in many other instances—especially cases where a person twists or extends something essentially true—the lies may go unchallenged, particularly if you have a high degree of trust in the person uttering them.

This chapter prepares you to spot deception by familiarizing you with flavors of lies and liars. It provides important background for using the techniques described later.

3. Are men and women different?

The corpus callosum is a thick bundle of nerves that joins the two hemispheres of the brain together. To put it in simple terms, men have a little one and women have a big one. In women, the development of this band of nerves enables fluctuation from left brain to right and back again at lightning speed. In contrast, men get sort of stuck. They use the left. Stop. They use the right. Stop. The effect is that men seem to persist in a logic pattern or a creative mode, while women might agilely flash back and forth.

This is one of the many factors explored in this chapter that underlies the reality that men and women are different

a. As interrogators, and

b. As liars

Another factor is that men and women have different stress mannerisms, that is, they have different ways of touching parts of their body, as well as ways that parts of their body react involuntarily to stress.

The chapter also covers the fact that brain development sets the under-30 crowd apart from adults in terms of deception.

Section II: Tools

4. Planning and Preparation

This chapter presents the elements that must come together in order for you to apply stress and extract information. Chief among them are

Rituals – yours and theirs. This refers simply to ways of doing things that you repeat. It could be an automatic response pattern or it could be something you do quite thoughtfully.

Roles. What will you project to the person you want a straight answer from? How do you want to be perceived? Are you playing mother? Tyrant? Seducer? Analyst? What is the other person's role?

Background information on your source. There is no such thing as irrelevant information.

Costume and scenery. All the world's a stage! What you wear, what's hanging on the walls, and how bright the lights are figure into your ability to accomplish your mission of detecting deception and getting at the truth.

5. Baselining to Detect and Apply Stress

Studies indicate that about 85 percent of people think they can spot a liar, but they can't! The cues they rely on may be valid for some people, and invalid for others. There is a great deal of physiology involved in lying, and to get a high degree of certainly about whether or not you've detected a lie, you first have to baseline your source.

This chapter gives the step-by-step process involved in setting the baseline through

Facial signs

Body signs

Auditory signals

Trappings, such as pictures on the wall and clothing, and

Rituals, to establish norms before applying stress

6. Extracting Information

The short answer to "how do you extract information without beating it out of someone" (which may not work anyway) is this: Get the person into limbic mode. At that point, the liar will create his own undoing. As a corollary, we might say that the most powerful thing you can do is find out what hurts the person the most—what that person will hurt *himself* over.

This chapter brings to life the process of moving the person into limbic mode. Clinically speaking, the limbic system has responsibility for your emotional state. It filters events emotionally rather than logically, stores highly charged emotional memories, modulates motivation, controls your appetite and sleep cycles, and affects your sex drive. The limbic system is responsible for fight or flight. Limbic memory can be trained.

In this chapter, readers explore approaches to moving someone into limbic mode. It includes the use of canned questions that come out of the exercises on baselining and how to use a technique called "minimalizing."

Section III: Applying the Tools in Love

Through scenarios and specific examples, the reader learns to put the techniques to work in a personal relationship.

7. Fight to get what you want

We've already established that different people and situations demand different approaches—that's the value of baselining. In the heat of the moment you are confronting someone, it's important to watch the signs so that the encounter moves in the direction you intend. Does the person you're addressing need more physical space at the moment, or will you get closer to your goal by actually invading his space? This is one of the many types of issues that the chapter explores.

8. Extract the truth

Sales professionals call it "the close." This is the moment when you get what you came for. How do you know you're there?

9. *Change the way you fight to make the relationship better*

Getting someone into a limbic mode is powerful, and not necessarily a set up for one man's (or woman's) victory, and another man's defeat. In the heat of a confrontation, people commonly say nasty things to each because they want to hit a soft spot. Your awareness of roles, trappings, facial signs, and more and can equip you to avoid the pitfalls of fighting that make it fruitless. You can change the tone, and outcome, of a fight with the one you love.

10. *Are you in captivity, not love?*

This chapter guides the reader through tough questions: Are you allowing your spouse or partner to lie because it's part of the *status quo*? Is it possible you're interpreting abusive behavior as love?

People in captivity, such as prisoners of war, commonly go to extremes to stabilize their environment as a way of maintaining their sanity. They tell themselves the treatment isn't so bad, perhaps even thinking that their captors are kind. In an abusive relationship, men and women can do the same thing.

By going through the process of baselining, of examining roles and rituals, and more, a person whose relationship is, in fact, captivity might be better equipped to recognize signs and seek help.

Section IV: Applying the Tools to Business

Through scenarios and specific examples, the

reader learns to put the techniques to work in a business relationship.

11. Direct a job interview

From both the point of view of an interviewer and an interviewee, the reader will see how the use of barriers, the trappings of wardrobe and wall hangings, and style of questions can produce advantages.

12. Get the upper hand in a meeting

Whether the meeting is with people you know well or with total strangers can be a big determining factor in knowing how to prepare and what to look for in terms of behavior. The purposes of the meeting also figure into the scenario.

This chapter reinforces the concept that you are on stage in a business meeting, just as a professional interrogator is on stage when she's breaking down a source. Interrogation is a performance art for an audience of one. A business meeting may have an audience of one, up close and personal, or it may involve many. Regardless of the size, you play a role that you must prepare for by having certain background information, among other things. And what if you don't have that information? What if people use jargon or throw unexpected questions at you? One of the techniques exposed in this chapter is how to use self-deprecation as a powerful tool to give you the upper hand.

13. Close the deal or make the sale

In this chapter, the scenarios and examples focus on the range of sales "interrogations" (that is, getting the answer you need and want), from effective cold calling, to building on a prior contact, to leveraging a ongoing relationship.

Section V: Self-Defense

14. How to avoid falling for these techniques

When you start to feel an emotion—a sign that you are creeping into limbic mode—you can pull up certain kinds of visual memories to back away from an emotional state. That's just one of the many techniques the chapter explores to protect you from falling for the ploys of interrogation.

Ah, but then there are the "counter-self-defense" moves! This includes ways of detecting whether someone is taking extraordinary measures to block your skills.

Conclusion: Respect your new power

Soldiers under interrogation have the advantage of being in a surreal environment. When you use the techniques in this book with people you love or work with, you are in the real world. It's not a world that you will leave behind when you're released from prison or when your tour of duty ends. It is *your* very real world with these same people in your face, and you in theirs, on a regular basis. So be careful.

This chapter helps the reader put the information into perspective. It poses tough questions and offers straightforward guidance. For example: If you're analyzing a person in terms of truth, perhaps you don't need that person in your life.

The last section of the proposal is roughly 20-30 pages of sample material from the proposed book. It is a chapter—more or less—depending on how long or short your chapters are.

I will say this now and then again later: Make the sample manuscript material an example of your best writing. Do not arbitrarily choose the first chapter of the book. When I sold my first book my sample chapter was number four—gun fire, non-healing wounds, high technology, corrupt politics. Much better than the first chapter.

To bring the reality of what that proposal meant to us in the long run—and I stress that I did make changes to protect our intellectual property—I want to give you the table of the contents for the book that came out of it: ***How to Spot a Liar***, first published by Career Press in 2005, and the published as a revised edition in 2012.

Introduction: Why You Need This Book

Section I: Context

Chapter 1: Where Do These Techniques Come From? (Or, What Does Abu Ghraib Have to Do with You?)

Chapter 2: Why and How People Lie

Chapter 3: Are Men, Women, and Children Different?

Section II: Tools

Chapter 4: Planning and Preparation

Chapter 5: Baselining to Detect and Apply Stress

Chapter 6: Extracting Information

Section III: Applying the Tools

Chapter 4: Overview

The Overview of your proposal is a page or two that provides an engaging introduction to your project. By "project," I mean not only your book, but also the marketing components of your publishing effort.

Roughly half of the submissions I get reflect a misperception of what the Overview should contain—even after the authors have seen the sample proposal. Particularly, authors of memoirs and true crime books often assume that the Overview should be a synopsis of the manuscript. If you think a synopsis will help sell the project, put one in. Just label it "synopsis," and make it a subset of the Overview. We are not in the "good old days" of the twentieth century when a memoir or true crime book could be pitched like fiction, that is, on the basis of the story alone without a case to support the marketing merits of the work and ability of the author to drive sales.

An Overview contains the following:

- A brief description of your book

- The compelling reason(s) why a market exists for this book

- A clear presentation of why you are the best person to write the book

- Any other facts or features that distinguish the project

Lead with your strongest point. In the sample proposal featured in Chapter 3, the first sentence establishes Greg as an international expert in interrogation. A top-flight interrogator sounds like someone who can teach you how to "make them tell the truth." I'm not saying this is a perfect beginning, but it's a solid opening punch.

One of the most common approaches to the first sentence is to tell the reader (in this case, the agent or editor) exactly what she already knows—and that's a bad start. Here are two examples:

- "Women buy stories of other women in transition, as the sales of *Eat Pray Love*—now topping 12 million—have shown." What does that tell me about your project? Nothing relevant. At that moment, I have a strong urge to stop reading.

- "Workplaces are profoundly affected by the COVID-19 pandemic." Really? Do you think that every agent and editor on the planet doesn't know that?

In your Overview, *it is your job to tell us what we don't know,* not to affirm or reinforce what we already know.

Many authors writing self-help/how-to books come to me because most of my own fit into that category. Whether one might best describe their selling point as a formula, method, or step-by-step process, they are asserting they have something unique, something new.

If you have a self-help/how-to book, it's often best to start with proof that your formula, method, or process actually works. Opening with, "I have a unique approach to weight loss" arouses skepticism. Instead, tell me a true story about someone you helped. In a paragraph, give me a taste of the real effects on a human being of what your unique weight-loss program can accomplish. Or if you can follow "I have a unique approach" with "and so far, 1,000 clients have lost a combined total of 19 tons," then I would read on.

You will get a better sense of the other pieces of the Overview after reading the other chapters in this section. Essentially, you will take your most powerful points in other parts of the proposal and put them into the Overview.

Regarding the final point—other facts or features that distinguish the project—you want to spotlight any fact that could immediately make the difference between deal and no deal. For example, state upfront if an A-list Hollywood celebrity has offered to write the Foreword for your book. Maybe you've won a Nobel Prize or been on *Good Morning America*; those facts are clearly worth noting.

Other distinguishing facts might be that you are CEO of a large company, or that you are a speaker/ author who gives 35 presentations a year to audiences ranging in size from 100 to 2,000. Yes, these are things that will show up again in your bio and/or promotion plan, but they are eye-catching statements that should be made in your Overview as well.

Chapter 5: The Market

In a page or two, provide a description of your primary market and any strong secondary markets. Depending on how it's written, a book on innovations in weaponry could appeal to a broad audience of people interested in military affairs and current events. Maybe anyone who is a member of the National Rifle Association would find it interesting. On the other hand, your style and content might make it appealing solely to engineers or nuclear physicists.

If you have designed the book for a broad audience, perhaps a secondary audience is students in international relations programs; the book might fit well on a recommended reading list. A technical book on weapons could also have a student audience, of course. But be careful in asserting that a good secondary market lies in a university population: Unless you have a plan to reach those people through presentations or professional connections, mentioning them sounds like you're padding.

In addition to your narrative description you can add the following:

- Numbers can be useful if the market is mainly a defined group, for example, left-handed people

- As support for those numbers, if the target group is extremely likely to be subscribers to a particular publication, such as *Psychology Today*, then include the size of the subscription base.

Common mistakes involve overestimating or

underestimating the market size by giving a description that is unbelievably broad or extremely specific.

If you go back and look at The Market section of the sample proposal, you will see some rather sweeping statements about who would be interested in this book, but they are shaped by references to cheating husbands and business deals. The fact is, a book about how to catch a liar and find the truth is a book that potentially appeals to everyone but cloistered nuns. Sales of the book, later published with the title *How to Spot a Liar* (Career Press), indicate that we were justified in making those sweeping statements: The market for his book has proven to be huge. After selling briskly for seven years, the book was revised and re-released in 2012.

A memoir by a middle-aged woman about a series of broken relationships may not have that kind of audience, however. First of all, it would be females of a certain age who would be the likely target. It would be a mistake to start off an analysis of the market by saying, "Anyone who's ever been in love would find this book appealing."

In contrast to such overestimations, many people think small. I commonly get proposals about a person battling a rare disease and the author describes the market as all 1,432 people in the United States who also have the disease. My response: Self-publish the book and sell it to those people because they should be very easy to find.

One of my authors, Vanessa Vega, did not make this mistake. She was a cutter who wanted to share the emotional pain that drove her to self-abuse as well as the journey toward healing. In her section on the market, Vanessa stated the following, and provided evidence to back it up: "The (sales) numbers illustrate that individuals are seeking out stories, written by real people struggling with disorders..." If she had painted herself into a corner by offering numbers on cutters instead of sales numbers on comparable books, she would have dramatically changed the perception of who would read *Comes the Darkness, Comes the Light* (AMACOM). By the way, it received a wonderful review from *Publisher's Weekly* when it came out in 2007.

Another tip on what you insert in your section on the market: Be mindful of your personal and professional connections. Earlier, I cautioned you about targeting an audience you don't know how to reach. As a corollary, when you leverage the connections you do have, perhaps you have an audience the publisher wouldn't have even considered unless you called it out. For example, perhaps you have national prominence in a large sorority like Delta Delta Delta. Because you are a sister, it's not unreasonable to assume that other sisters would buy your book just because of that affiliation.

One of my star clients was Ira Neimark, the former CEO of Bergdorf Goodman in New York. Needless to say, he noted that his target market for his memoir with business lessons, *The Rise of Fashion* (Fairchild), included shoppers at BG. Not surprisingly, that memoir as well as his first one, *Crossing Fifth Avenue to Bergdorf Goodman,* are strong sellers at BG even after his death in April 2019.

Chapter 6: Promotion Plan/ Platform

Your promotion plan is the expression of how you will reach the target audiences you described in The Market. Your past experience as a speaker, expert source for media, writer of articles and blogs, social networking, and related achievements are all relevant. In addition to reading this chapter, I urge you to plunge into the final section of this book, which explores how to implement a promotion plan once you have a contract with a publisher.

People sometimes "scream" at me in their emails because I ask them to try their best to put a promotion plan together. My intent is to challenge their imagination about what they are capable of doing to reach their target audience, but the invitation to commit to "getting out there" often elicits resentment, or even anger.

Their emails look like this—and these are examples of how real people really vent at me:

Isn't this the PUBLISHER'S responsibility? Why would they even print my book if THEY weren't going to promote it?

I'm a doctor, not a PR PERSON! I read your bio, you're a former PR PERSON, so you write this section.

How do you expect a FULL-TIME MOM to write a book AND figure out how to promote it?

*What are you saying? That I have to spend my
retirement money on a pricey New York publicist?
Are you NUTS?!?*

I don't ask for a promotion plan just to make
your intestines knot up, so please don't scream at me.
Here is a letter I send everyone from whom I invite a
proposal, unless that person has already made it clear
that he or she has a background in promotion:

Dear (Author),

I'm writing this letter because there is a
misunderstanding about what this agency and
many publishers are looking for in a non-fiction
project.

As an author myself, I have great respect for
talent, and I wish that I could find a publishing
house for every gifted writer who approaches me.
I would have steady, abundant cash flow—but I
would be making money from advances against
royalties, rather than actual sales. That's that
kind of thing that wasn't uncommon in the good
ol' days.

Well now, we're in the good new days and
your talent is only a little piece of the deal. Once
you have a deal, you will be expected to work
aggressively to help promote your book, not only
to earn whatever advance you get, but also to
make your project profitable. Your book has to
have a sizable audience willing to spend money
on what you wrote and you have to know how

to reach that audience.

The simple message is this: Publishing is a business and there is no shame in it becoming an even better business. If you want to be part of it, then you are a good fit for this agency. We will be your active partner in making your book a financial success. If you want to "just write," however, then please do us both a favor and go somewhere else.

After reading this letter, if you believe you can make a strong business case for your book, then submit your proposal to me.

Try to think of the business part of writing as integral to keeping your passion for writing alive.

Sincerely, Maryann

I thought that was respectful and helpful and cannot fully comprehend why someone would "scream" at me after reading it. To prevent any further outbreaks, which hurt my feelings, I will walk you through the Promotion section of your proposal.

The essential things to note are these:

- The promotion section can be as many pages as it takes to make your case, within reason.

I worked with a physician-psychologist team that had tremendous visibility in the community of alternative medicine caregivers, as well as respect in the mainstream medical community. Their promotion plan included presentations, media appearances, and publications that took six pages. And that was just the past couple of years.

Those items are relevant, but consider ways to group them. If your have had five papers in the *American Journal of Psychology*, then group them together. Don't necessarily be bound by dates and list them as you would in a CV. And if you have appeared as an expert commentator on a CNN show five times, then again, group them. The impact will be greater than separating them.

- Your plan for how to reach the people you described in The Market is the core of this section.

I am very sympathetic to the author who says, "I don't know how to do a promotion plan. Please guide me." That cry for help was one of the principle reasons for writing this book.

At this point, it may be helpful to tell you the story of how I laid the foundation of my corporate career in promotion. I was 22 years old and working in a two-person office as an administrative assistant to the executive director of a small agricultural trade association. I caught my boss embezzling and reported my findings to the chairman of the board. He fired my boss immediately, took me out to dinner, and said essentially this: "You're smart. You're dedicated. We appreciate you. Please take over until we find a replacement." I knew it was time to do a membership renewal campaign, so I took the "please take over" part very seriously. After reading some articles about what colors made people feel happy and how it was important to personalize solicitations, I mailed pink renewal cards with personal letters to every one of the small and corporate farmers on our list of about 800. Yes, the cards were pink and they went to farmers or agribusiness executives. For whatever reason, the rate of return I got on those renewals surpassed previous years—by a lot. When my new boss arrived three months later, I had established myself as a marketing guru to agricultural employers.

My point is this: I used my imagination, combined it with research, and took a risk. That's what promotion is all about.

So in your promotion plan, explore the possibilities of what you can really do to reach your target audiences. What can your club memberships, professional associations, church affiliations, family and friends do for you—no, what *will* they do for you? Whom do you know in the media?

Just being willing to show up for a book signing or TV appearance scheduled by your publisher is meaningless. The publisher assumes you will be willing to do that. The important statement is what you can do on your own.

- Be explicit about your experience as a speaker, previous media exposure, other published works, presence on social networks, ties to celebrities (even if they are only celebrities in your subject area), and high-profile people who could be counted on to write a Foreword or endorsement for your book. Better yet, go to the person(s) you've targeted to write your Foreword and endorsements beforehand and see if you can get at least a one-line commitment to help, or that they will consider providing the Foreword or endorsement after they read your manuscript.

Chapter 7: Competitive Analysis

Even seasoned authors have trouble with this, so your confusion puts you in good company.

Remember those people you described in The Market and talked about reaching in your Promotion Plan/Platform? Here is the section of your proposal in which you state what they are buying. You also explain briefly why they would buy your book in addition to, or instead of, those books.

Your competitive analysis positions your book in the marketplace. It illustrates that your book has a market.

Common mistakes are these—and this is a list that keeps getting longer:

• Arguing "There are no comparables." In most cases, that's like saying, "There is no market." You may be the only person on the planet who has had personal contact with extraterrestrial beings and has proof of it, but your book about that experience has comparables. The millions of us who subscribe to *National Geographic* and read the December 2009 cover article entitled "Are We Alone?" are very possibly reading books that cover the topic, too. What are those books? Not the books by crackpots, but the books by scientists.

• Listing bad books with bad track records. Why would a publisher be thrilled to take on your book when the only books you can compare it to, or contrast it with, are bad books that sold less than 5,000 copies? Mentioning a flawed book that has certain popularity *is* fine, however, because it suggests that readers are interested in the topic.

• Emphasizing popular books that have become clichés. As I noted earlier, authors pitch a lot of self-help projects to me. Would you venture a guess as to how many authors compared their book to Rhonda Byrne's *The Secret* every year for the first few years after its release? About 50. The number dropped by 2011. After Elizabeth Gilbert's *Eat Pray Love* came out in 2006, female memoirists (and even a few men) kept putting it in as a comp. When it fits, use it, but don't shoe-horn a bestseller into your competitive analysis in an attempt to suggest your book will be as popular as that one.

• Providing a long list of books, but no indication of whether they are better or worse, and how one might arrive at that conclusion.

• Mixing genres. You're a physician who has a book with a central, dramatic story about your pioneering research in medical nanotechnology. In your competitive analysis, you list four other memoirs by physicians, a couple of novels on related subjects, three books on medical technology, and a current events book on the state of federal funding for medical research. In a way, that's not completely ridiculous, but you need to organize your material in such a way that your book is clearly positioned. If you have a memoir, then your main comps are memoirs. Nonetheless, mentioning the others in a sub-section can provide valuable insight about the content of your book and your perceived appeal to the target audiences. If you mention the current events book that covers funding for R&D, the presumption is that your book covers the subject, albeit from a personal point of view. Be careful about doing this, however. In this example, the author's citing three books on medical technology suggests that a core part of the book is technology-oriented. Acquisitions editors considering a memoir could find that a turn-off.

One of the authors I worked with had an extremely hard time with the content of his competitive analysis. I contacted a few editor friends and asked them casually what they thought of the project. They all zeroed in on the competitive analysis and declared the book "regional" and therefore not something they would be interested in.

Through his competitive analysis, the author had positioned his project as belonging to a collection of works by New Yorkers for New Yorkers. The editors' conclusion that the book had only regional appeal made perfect sense. But I knew that people beyond the boroughs would find the content interesting, too, and so I tried to get the author to expand his vision of what constituted a competitive book. Here is an email to him:

What do *The Female Brain*, *Outliers*, and *A Whole New Mind* have in common? They are all about how people think and behave and why they think and behave that way. I have read all three, and many more like them, because I am interested in the subject of human behavior.

A good competitive analysis makes it clear, in both a specific and a broad sense, what books your target audience would buy in addition to or instead of yours. In the above instance, a proposal for *The Female Brain* might indicate that the specific audience is well educated women who enjoy reading about neurobiology. That describes me. But it would also indicate that the broad audience is any reader who finds human behavior intriguing, as evidenced by other books they are reading such as.... You get the picture—yes?

If your book will appeal only to people who enjoy high-brow controversy about arcane scientific matters related to the heritage of African-American New Yorkers, then you have an audience of about 230 people. Unless you can come up with a competitive analysis that shows that millions of people might potentially be interested in this book, then you do not have a book that a mainstream commercial publisher is interested in.

Chapter 8: Author Bio

When I finish reading your bio, I want to leap out of my chair and exclaim: "This is the perfect person to write this book!"

Your credentials need to be obvious, but don't just insert a résumé or curriculum vitae. If yours is really impressive, then go ahead and add it as an appendix to the proposal. Do not stick a nine-page CV into the body of your proposal. It disrupts the entire flow. Remember: Some editors will want to sit down and read the entire document from beginning to end, so keep excessive details out of the body of your proposal.

Start your bio with the most important fact about yourself as it relates to the book. Here are real first sentences from five of my authors' bios. Match the sentences to the titles that follow them:

1. Christopher Byrne (aka "The Toy Guy") is one of the toy industry's leading experts and a frequent guest on national TV.

2. Lena Sisco is a former military intelligence officer and interrogator and a well-known expert in deceptive analysis.

3. Aviva Klompas served as the director of Speechwriting for Israel's Permanent Mission to the United Nations in New York City.

4. Peter Earnest worked in the Central Intelligence Agency for 36 years, including a quarter-century in the Agency's National Clandestine Service.

5. Robert Kaluza was a senior engineer aboard Deepwater Horizon when it exploded in 2010, killing 11 men.

- *Speaking for Israel*
- *Deepwater Deception*
- *You're Lying!*
- *Business Confidential*
- *Toy Time!*

The answers are 1-e, 2-c, 3-a, 4-d, and 5-b.

Obvious. As it should be.

Chapter 9: Table of Contents, Chapter Synopses, and Sample Material

The editorial portion of your proposal comprises three sections: table of contents, chapter-by-chapter synopsis, and sample manuscript material

The TOC

Your goal is to make the table of contents like a fabulous first date. I see you. I'm curious about you. I want to be near you. Tell me more about you.

For a how-to book, state the promises. Whether it's a nine-step process to achieve sexual bliss, or ten things you must do to spot a liar, put the promise in the chapter titles. If you are too clever, your reader will not see what you have to offer.

With narrative non-fiction like a memoir or true crime book, pull the reader along with your chapter titles. Here is how Mary Kinney Branson and Jack Branson skillfully did this with their true crime book, *Murder in Mayberry* (New Horizon)—and this is just the chapters in "Part 1: Ann's Murder":

Blood Ties

Something Terrible

A Promise

Searching for a Killer

A Bloody Scenario

Stress Grows

Who's the Killer?

The Nightmare Continues

The Parade Begins

Bloodstains

Viewing the Body

Suspects and Other Mourners

Graveside

In the Valley

Just reading these opening chapter titles creates a sense of tension and movement. In addition, because the book contains five parts, it's clear at the outset that the chapters will be bite-sized. The table of contents therefore serves as an invitation to put the bed on your nightstand and read a little every night and every morning.

Now consider the chapter titles of a how-to book on project management. This is how Jackie Jenkins-Scott grabs the bookstore browser with her table of contents for *The 7 Secrets of Responsive Leadership* (Career Press/Red Wheel Weiser, 2020):

Introduction: The Nature of Responsive Leadership

Chapter 1: Secret 1—Take Advantage of Opportunity

Chapter 2: Secret 2—Compete Well by Leading with Heart

Chapter 3: Secret 3—Keep Your Bags Packed

Chapter 4: Secret 4—Stay on Point in the Midst of Risk

Chapter 5: Secret 5—Move Your Opposition

Be clever, but clear. Catchy, but not obtuse. Consider your table of contents an important part of marketing your book.

The Chapter-by-Chapter Synopsis

The section following the TOC provides a little detail about each chapter. The purpose is twofold:

• Demonstrate you have a firm grasp of the content of the entire book, not just an idea for a whole book and a sense of what a chapter or two will look like.

• Spotlight the flow of the book. Whether your book is a narrative or a set of step-by-step instructions, you want to make it clear how one chapter flows to the next and keeps the reader interested.

There is no need to be detailed; the need is to be clear about the main point(s) in each chapter. Going back to the TOC for Jackie's book, consider how she described the contents of Chapter 1, combining a snippet of a story with the business lessons the chapter offered:

Chapter 1: Take advantage of opportunity

At its core, this book is about the intimate relationship between leadership and opportunity, so this opening chapter is about the identification and timing of opportunity:

- What constitutes a good opportunity?

- When is a desirable time to take advantage of a good opportunity?

There was one vacant lot left on our ten-acre campus at Dimock. We'd already been told by an appraiser that the best use of the campus, which was ten minutes from downtown Boston, was to tear down the dilapidated structures and build condos. Building condos would not contribute to long-term sustainability of an inner-city community health care center, though.

I knew the land must represent some kind of opportunity, but what was it?

My primary consideration had to be how the action we took would enhance the services to the community we served. We already provided a range of healthcare services, so the question became—what else did they need that we could be in a position to provide? What could we put there to give our target audience more of a "one-stop shopping" experience?

People living in inner cities who are impoverished or barely making it need access to welfare services. So our answer to "what to do?" emerged in response to that need: build a new facility for the welfare department.

It brought families to the campus who had never been there and saved them the aggravation of running to multiple places for the services they required. It also gave us rent money as well as some additional grant money that we could apply to other programs at Dimock.

The steps to identifying that this was an ideal opportunity are part of the guidance in this chapter.

Then there is the issue of timing. Opportunities can be like the weather in Rapid City, South Dakota, which has the most unpredictable weather in the United States according to National Geographic.

First, it might hit you without warning. After observing it briefly and finding it interesting, you collect what you believe to be relevant data so you understand the phenomenon and try to answer basic questions: How long will it last? How powerful is it? Why did this occur now? What's the significance of my going into the middle of it?

One skill a responsive leader must have is that of being able to ascertain the best moment to seize an opportunity. It's a Goldilocks issue: the porridge can't be too hot or too cold.

In addition to major, career changing opportunities that come along, once you are in a position of leadership, you need the same skills of identification and timing to determine how to pick your priorities.

One thing you may have noticed is that the chapter title in the proposal didn't exactly match the final title because the publisher had not decided to call the book *The 7 Secrets* until later in the process. In many cases, the number of chapters, names of them, content organization, and other elements of the book will also evolve after a publisher decides to acquire a book.

Sample Manuscript Material

The sample manuscript material you choose to put into the proposal must be your best work. I can understand why a lot of authors submit Chapter 1: Either (a) they haven't written anything else, or (b) they feel the reader needs the set-up material in Chapter 1 to understand the rest of the book.

Unfortunately, the Introduction or Chapter 1 of a book is often expository in nature, a prelude to the meaty material. Do yourself a favor: Keep writing and then send something that hits high editorial standards. That may end up being Chapter 1, but don't assume that the agent wants to see Chapter 1 by default. I'd much rather see a sample chapter I may not fully understand but one that hits the sky when it comes to editorial merits.

With a proposal completed, you take a giant step toward commercial publishing. After your document is reviewed favorably and you're offered a contract, then the hard work really begins, whether or not you already have a complete draft of the work you're proposing.

Part III: The Contract

Chapter 10: What an Agent Does for You

As soon as your agent shows serious interest in your book, she's thinking about matching you with a publishing house. Her greatest value is not in identifying good candidates, though; it is in knowing which editors to approach at those houses.

She will pitch your project in an email, by phone, or in a face-to-face meeting, but mostly by email. Nearly everything we do in terms of supplying material for review by a publisher is done electronically, although I admit I really enjoy meeting with editors and letting my passion for a project radiate.

When an editor invites a proposal in response to the pitch, we are on our way.

Just as I told you earlier that you need to respond specifically to an agent's guidelines on a proposal, I have to respond specifically to a publisher's guidelines. If a publisher issues new guidelines that require three full chapters with a proposal, I may need to come back to you to expand your sample material. Some want an estimated completion date for the manuscript. I would need to come back to you and find out when that would be. When I ask that question, here's the wrong answer: "It depends on how much money they give me."

As you can see, in doing my job, I might be making more work for you. Expect it.

Depending on the type of project, I may go to lots of publishers, or the number might be extremely limited. I had one project that I took on because I immediately thought, "This is perfect for an editor I know at Random

House." Frankly, if the editor at Penguin Random House had said, "Not interested," I would have wondered if I were in the right profession.

In short, the first big thing your agent does for you after helping you clean up your proposal is finding a publisher that welcomes your book with open arms.

The Right Publisher

As I begin the process of identifying the publishing houses that are logical candidates for a book, authors frequently want to know the criteria for selection. They usually assume I will go straight for Big Advance, which is synonymous with Big Publisher. That's a joke, by the way, because Big Advance is not synonymous with Big Publisher. I've seen some puny advances come from big houses and some reasonably generous advances come from mid-sized houses.

- I look for a publisher that
- Wants books like this.
- Is currently making deals for books like this.
- Does well with books like this.
- Provides follow-on support for titles in the areas of promotion, foreign rights, audio rights, and so on.
- Has reasonable terms and conditions.

When all of those factors come together and I get the pleasure of pitching to an editor I enjoy working with, then it's a happy day.

The Offer

A talented young client once announced to me that he would like a six-figure advance. I assured him that he would get a six-figure advance—on his second book, after his first book hit the bestseller lists.

For his first book, I got him $8,000 up front; he was crestfallen. He wanted at least ten times that amount.

The publisher produced a beautiful book, and my author earned glowing reviews. The publisher and author jointly promoted the book fairly well. And at the end of the first year of sales, the author's earnings were ($4,700). Yes, that is a negative number. His book had earned $3,300 through sales and he was, as we say, upside down in terms of his advance.

As an agent, I'm sitting in the middle between a publisher that aims to make a profit and an author who wants the financial rewards associated with writing a good book. I try to negotiate the best deal I can for my author, but I want both parties to win. It doesn't do me a bit of good if publishers go out of business.

The truth is that there is no financial reward necessarily associated with writing a good book. When you get an offer, the publisher has calculated how many copies the book will likely sell in a given period. Your ability to promote and the gut feelings of the publisher's marketing team affect that number. On the basis of the calculation, the publisher makes an initial offer.

When a publisher makes an offer, it might be presented formally in a letter, casually in an email, or in a phone conversation. Most often, it's a phone call from an excited editor who wants to tell me the good news. Let's say the offer looks like this:

Advance: $8,000

Payout: 1/2 on signing of contract; 1/2 on delivery and acceptance of final manuscript.

Territory: World

Royalties: 10% of net receipts.

Electronic Royalties: 25% of net receipts

Subsidiary rights: 50/50

I've run my own numbers on the project, so I counter with something I think is more appropriate. That back and forth might end suddenly with agreement on the new terms, or like the car salesman on the showroom floor, the editor might excuse himself and say, "I have to find out how much wiggle room I have."

The terms and conditions of a contract deserve a book of their own, so the point I want to make here is that the above categories are just a small part of what the agent and editor will ultimately talk about. Even though there may be agreement on the advance and on percentages, the contract could be littered with issues such as the due date for the manuscript, how much the publisher will deduct from royalties for the index, who is responsible for paying for the illustrations, how many complimentary copies of the completed work the author will get, and on and on.

So one of the things your agent does for you is actually read the contract. As I was writing this chapter, I pulled out my files to see what the shortest and longest contracts were so you would get a sense of how the level of detail can vary. The shortest contract in my files was six 8 ½ x 11 inch pages. The longest was twenty-eight legal-sized pages.

Author Guidelines

When they send the executed contract, most publishers send guidelines so that you know how to set up the manuscript. They will often include permissions forms and specifications for artwork as well. You can seriously hamper the production process if you ignore this material.

Your agent will probably have a copy of it in her file, too, so if you lose it, just ask for a replacement.

Chapter 11: What to Expect after the Manuscript is Done

As an author, I've worked with twelve different publishers. My insights as an author are more valuable in this section than my insights as an agent because agents generally back off from the editorial/production process. I always do unless the author asks me for specific input on the manuscript or needs a deadline extension. I re-engage when the release date for the book is near and it's time to promote—the subject of the final chapter.

Although I have never encountered identical processes at different houses, I can tell you what to you expect in the most elaborate version I know. When your experience is simpler, you can be pleasantly surprised.

In most cases, these steps follow closely after the submission of your manuscript. Your manuscript should now be associated with a specific timeline and both you and the editors you work with need to stick to that timeline.

- Macro edits – Your first editor, who may or may not be the acquisitions editor for your book, will read through your manuscript. He will pose questions, recommend structural changes, and address other big-picture issues.

    - You will respond with a revision in a given period of time. If there are some significant issues, you might get thirty days. Commonly, it's as little as two weeks. If you have a full-time job while you are under contract to produce a book, you will either need to take vacation days when you get your production schedule or hope that your employer doesn't catch you working on edits at the office. If she does, offer to dedicate the book to her if she doesn't fire you.

• Line edits – Your next editor will go line-by-line and correct your grammar, recommend different word choices, pose specific questions about the meaning of statements, and challenge your logic if necessary.

• Again, you'll probably get two weeks.

• Permissions check – If you have included quotes or cited concepts that came from another source, you will need to prove that you have permission to use them.

• The turn-around time on this will probably be a day or two. After all, this is something that should have been handled upfront. The publisher will have supplied you with permissions forms with the guidelines that came with the contract.

• Illustrations/photo placement – Your manuscript will be words with references to figures that will be inserted in production.

• Depending on how many images you have in your manuscript, the process of labeling and captioning can be extremely time-consuming.

• Copy edits – Your next editor will clean up the remaining mess, such as misplaced commas and typos.

• When you get the page proofs, there

should be almost nothing to change unless lines or words have been inadvertently dropped out. I have seen this happen in about half the books I've done, so beware. For that reason, you need to read every line of the manuscript once again.

One final note about content: In your acknowledgments, remember all of the people who did all of those edits and helped you sort through your artwork and permissions. Your book includes a part of them, too. Thank them.

Part IV: Promotion is Part of Publishing —Tips and Tricks

According to my Myers-Briggs profile, I'm an introvert, although I have the ability to push myself into the spotlight—and I quite like it. Most of the authors I represent are also introverts. Theoretically, it's harder for introverts to do promotion than it is for extroverts, but I don't think that has to be true. We will not be the extroverted authors juggling our books on the street corner to attract TV cameras and crowds, but we may be the ones who choose effective routes like blogging and writing articles.

In this section, I will

- Give a little background on why you need to think about promotion in advance of the publication of your book.

- Offer you tips and tricks to get started right now, so that by the time you approach an agent, you will have the basics in place.

- Provide pointers about what to do just before your book is released, as well as in the weeks and years after its release.

The Requirement to Promote

Authors commonly tell me, "I'll be available for any interview the publisher arranges," or "No matter what it takes, I'll respond to every media request the publisher wants me to handle."

Adopt that attitude, and you will probably fail as an author. Your wonderful book will hit 3,000 in sales if you are very, very lucky—unless you combine that desire with aggressive promotion.

I am not slandering publishers when I say that, in most cases, they can't afford to hire a publicist for you. A staff publicist might be handling five or six launches at one time and you may be lucky to get a sliver of that person's time. Publishing is a business that operates on tight margins. The reason that someone like Dr. Mary L. Trump gets a multi-million dollar advance and a substantial investment from the publisher in publicity is that—you know the answer—millions of people are dying to read what she has to say about her uncle in the White House before she even says it. They pre-order her book well in advance of its official release. The publisher is making a smart investment by paying professionals to help drive book sales and buzz, and the result will be worth far more than they paid her upfront.

So, unless you are a celebrity, as you send out your query letters to agents, be mindful of the requirement to promote your own book.

Implement Your Plan—I Mean <u>Now</u>

It doesn't matter what genre of non-fiction book you have already written or propose to write, it contains information that can be used in presentations, on an informational and/or entertaining website, in a blog or articles, in YouTube videos, and on Facebook pages. Use your imagination.

Here's an exercise to get you started:

Part 1: You've been asked to do a 20-minute presentation about your book. All you have is a detailed outline of the book right now, but you know what the key points will be. Write down five points that could keep you talking—with substance—for 20 minutes. Let's use the example of the proposed book described in Chapter 3.

1. Baselining, a basic skill in detecting deception

2. Baselining eye movement

3. The role of the "big four" gestures

4. The significance of deviations from baseline

5. Deviations that make you wonder, "Is he lying?"

Part 2: Take 20 minutes out of your day and talk to yourself. Actually try to deliver a presentation in that time frame that follows your outline. Now ask yourself, "Who would be interested in hearing this?"

Part 3: Take one point in that outline and turn it into a 500-word article. When you were talking to yourself, didn't you say at least 500 words about one of the topics? Now ask yourself, "Which online or print publication would this article fit into very well?"

Part 4: Take that article and figure out how many tweets and blog postings you could get out of it. Now ask yourself, "Who wants to get those tweets and read that blog?"

Part 5: Go back to your original outline of a 20-minute presentation and imagine creating an entire website out of it. Now ask yourself, "What benefit would visitors to the site get out of it?"

Why would you do this exercise before your book is published—or even written? When you go through the exercise of figuring out how to promote a book that isn't even a book yet, you focus on your audience. You focus on the people who want to hear your message, your information, and your story.

Your book will be a better book *because you thought about how to promote it.*

Once you do the exercise, it's time to implement Parts 1 through 5. So, it's not really "just" an exercise after all. It's your pre-publication plan to raise your visibility and enhance your appeal as a non-fiction author. You need to make the presentations, write the article(s), post the tweets and blog entries, and set up your website.

You don't have to do this all yourself if you have the financial resources to hire a publicist, web designer, ghostwriter, and so on. If you have disposable income, a professional book publicist is a potentially great investment—but don't wait until the book has been out a month to hire her. Get your publicity team on board before you go to an agent and you will find yourself with far more options in terms of agent and publisher than if you wait.

Most of my authors don't have that kind of money. They take the DIY approach and usually exceed their wildest expectations because they care about what they've written.

If your material means a lot to you, you have a pervasive desire to find ways to share it—and that means through media other than your book.

Implement Your Plan—I Mean for <u>Years</u>

Do as many of these steps as you can, and let your publisher establish the timeframe for the pre-publication activities. I'm giving you estimates based on my personal experience.

- About six months before your book is published, collect endorsements. They should come from people whose names, or at least accomplishments, will be recognizable to your target audience. The endorsement list for Ira Neimark's first book, *Crossing Fifth Avenue to Bergdorf Goodman*, is a good mix of eye-catching titles and recognizable names—the ones that need no titles:

Calvin Klein

Leonard Lauder, Chairman of The Estée Lauder Companies

Donald J. Trump

Burton M. Tansky, CEO, Neiman Marcus Group

Allen Questrom, former CEO, Federated Department Stores and JC Penney

Jim Gold, President and CEO, Bergdorf Goodman

Jeffry Aronsson, former CEO, Oscar de la Renta and Donna Karan, International

Carla Fendi, President of the Board of Directors, The Fendi Group

- Establish a web presence. Whether you have a personal website on which you can feature you book, or a book-specific website, get set up. Your cover design should be available six-nine months in advance of the release of your book, but at the very latest, it should be available four months out. Publishers need the cover design and marketing copy in good order for their catalogues and sales teams. Use their designs and information, to which you probably contributed, on your website.

- Link to your publisher's site and/or to the booksellers they tell you to link to. This is very important: One way publishers maintain good relationships with booksellers is by ensuring that their authors link to booksellers' sites.

- Feature your blog on the site, if you can be a reliable blogger. All communications related to your web presence, such as blogging, tweeting, wall posts, and so on, are part of the fun of promoting your work. But you can't just post a blog on January 15, and then not even look at it again until April 4. You need to pay attention because these outgoing bursts of information invite incoming bursts of information. People expect you to pay attention to what their responses to you are.

- Place articles in online and print magazines and start the process six months in advance of your release date. I know it sounds old-fashioned to approach print publications, but it is not. Certain magazines have loyal readers and the magazines they enjoy tend to hand around the house for a long time. I savor *National Geographic* and read magazines as different as *Forbes, Departures,* and *Vogue*; I can only be satisfied by having that printed copy in my hands as I board an airplane or crawl into bed. Go to the websites of the publications that your target readers are likely to read regularly. Find out what the opportunities are for placement of an article that expands or summarizes a key piece of your book. The lead time on many of the major publications is long, so you need to start this process a minimum of six months in advance of the release date for your book. Be mindful that some of the publications will look for a news hook. For example, your relationship book might have material that would be great for the February issue of a magazine, but seem far less appealing when the same publication is focused on back-to-school products.

• Line up your media tools and start pitching. Never stop—this is one way to keep your book alive forever.

> • For example, Help a Report Out (HARO) is free and has gained traction over the years as a legitimate tool for experts to connect with journalists. Note well: Be laser-like in your responses to reporters' queries. These listings are serious requests from journalists for information to put into stories. Be specific about what expertise or experience you have to offer. I often respond with information about my clients' expertise. With their permission, I provide the journalist with a summary of a client's ability to contribute to the story, and then give the journalist contact information for my author. If that reporter spots gold, then fine. But it is not appropriate for me to either follow-up or to provide the client with contact information for the person writing the story.

> • Put together a list of print, broadcast, and online journalists (that includes bloggers and podcast hosts) who cover

your geographic area, as well as your area of expertise. The easy way to do this research is through services such as Cision. Unfortunately, most individuals would find that too pricey, so the alternative is to do it the hard way: by painstakingly researching all possibilities you can find on the web. Once you have your list, here is how you use it:

* Make contact when you have real news for them, or when you can advance a story they have written. Here's an example: One of your target journalists has written a story about the impact of wildfires in your area on homeowners. You are a botanist who has written a book about wildflowers. You could advance that story by offering information on what kind of wildflowers were destroyed, and how the wildflower population will be restored naturally or by man's intervention.

* Let your target journalists know why you are a good source for them—and be precise. If you're a physician, when you send your note, be specific about your expertise. For example, "I am a sleep specialist who can offer you tips on getting a good night's sleep, red flags for detecting serious sleep disorders, and advice on resolving problems with your spouse when it comes to sleeping habits."

* Monitor blog entries applicable to you and respond early and often. As long as the blog has legitimacy, the readers have a serious interest in the subject and discussions. They are your target audience, and they are also people who can help create buzz about your book.

• Write letters to the editor. With a tip of the hat to my old friend, Susan RoAne, I offer this advice I got from her. You probably read all kinds of print and online publications, so speak up when someone gets it right, gets it wrong, or misses a key point on which you're an expert.

• Exploit the possibilities of personal, electronic connections. Stated simply: Send emails to your friends about your book and ask them to pass those emails along. Give people the opportunity to celebrate your success.

• Every time you visit a bookstore, go meet the manager and offer to sign copies of your book. If the manager says, "We'd enjoy hosting a book signing," do it. You usually don't make much money at book signings, but they generate tremendous good will with the booksellers. Put your heart into it, even if only three people show up.

• Present at every opportunity. Most of us started out with Rotary Clubs that met at 7 AM. It was worth every minute of lost sleep to see faces light up when I talked about one of my books. And they bought my books; these audiences will be some of the best you will ever encounter. They appreciate you; you appreciate them. It's a love fest.

• For those of you who are professional speakers, I realize that you probably started at Rotary, too, but your agenda needs to be a robust speaking schedule with either advance, bulk purchases or back-of-room sales after the presentation. You should know the drill. If you don't, contact your local National Speakers Association chapter.

• Give yourself a party. I don't care what anyone says about launch parties, whether or not media attend. If people should have cake and champagne when they get married, they should have cake and champagne when their book is published. Do it. Do it right. You deserve a celebration!

Acknowledgments

Jim McCormick asked me why I was spending hours every month giving out free advice on how to do a proposal. His idea to do a little book led to the content here and I thank him for that. I also had amazing support from my colleague, Judith Bailey, who is now the Executive Editor of Armin Lear. Immense thanks to all the authors and editors who are in my world as well! You teach me daily and demand excellence from me.

Author Biography

Maryann Karinch began her career in book publishing in 1994 with the publication of her first work of non-fiction and has followed it with 30 other commercially published works. In 2004, Maryann founded The Rudy Agency, a literary agency specializing in non-fiction. With a background in marketing communications, she figured that this move built naturally on her skills. She never dreamed how much she would enjoy the challenge of representing literary talent—pitching ideas and products as she had done for corporations such as Apple and AT&T. And she was thrilled with the ability to connect with so many new authors and their books as well as the book-loving, author-loving editors who are the soul of publishing houses everywhere.

The Rudy Agency has placed the work of more than 150 authors with 49 different publishers during that time. Most of those authors were first timers, but they came in with a professional commitment to hit high editorial standards and promote their books--and those are the kind of authors who are the prime audience for her new book with Armin Lear, *Game Plan for Getting Published.*

After coaching many of her authors through the proposal writing process, and guiding them through the launch of their books, she decided to share the process she has taught them.